ENVIRONMENTAL ISSUES

ANIMALS IN DANGER

By Gemma McMullen

KidHaven
PUBLISHING

Published in 2017 by
KidHaven Publishing, an Imprint of Greenhaven Publishing, LLC
353 3rd Avenue
Suite 255
New York, NY 10010

Designer: Matt Rumbelow
Editor: Gemma McMullen

Cataloging-in-Publication Data

Names: McMullen, Gemma.
Title: Animals in danger / Gemma McMullen.
Description: New York : KidHaven Publishing, 2017. | Series: Environmental issues | Includes index.
Identifiers: ISBN 9781534520417 (pbk.) | ISBN 9781534520431 (library bound) | ISBN
9781534520424 (6 pack) | ISBN 9781534520448 (ebook)
Subjects: LCSH: Endangered species–Juvenile literature. | Wildlife conservation–Juvenile literature.
Classification: LCC QL83.M36 2017 | DDC 333.95'42–dc23

Printed in the United States of America

CPSIA compliance information: Batch #CW17KL: For further information contact Greenhaven Publishing LLC, New York, New York at 1-844-317-7404.

Please visit our website, www.greenhavenpublishing.com. For a free color catalog of all our
high-quality books, call toll free 1-844-317-7404 or fax 1-844-317-7405.

Words in **bold** can be found in the glossary on page 24.

CONTENTS

WHAT IS A HABITAT?

A habitat is the place where an animal lives. Almost every place on Earth is a habitat. Many different animals live in the same habitat. They rely on plants and each other for food. Animals' bodies are suited to the habitat in which they live.

WHY ARE HABITATS IN DANGER?

Habitats all over the world are being destroyed. Humans are destroying habitats by mistreating them or by taking them over for their own use. The number of animals living in endangered habitats is getting smaller, and some species have even become **extinct**.

THE RAIN FOREST

Rain forests are large areas of forest that are wet. The trees in a rain forest are very close together and are very tall. Most of the world's rain forests are tropical. This means they get a large amount of rainfall, they are warm, and the plants stay green all year.

Rain forests are home to over half of all the animal species that we know about, including monkeys, birds, bats, and butterflies.

DID YOU KNOW THAT NEW ANIMAL SPECIES ARE BEING DISCOVERED ALL THE TIME?

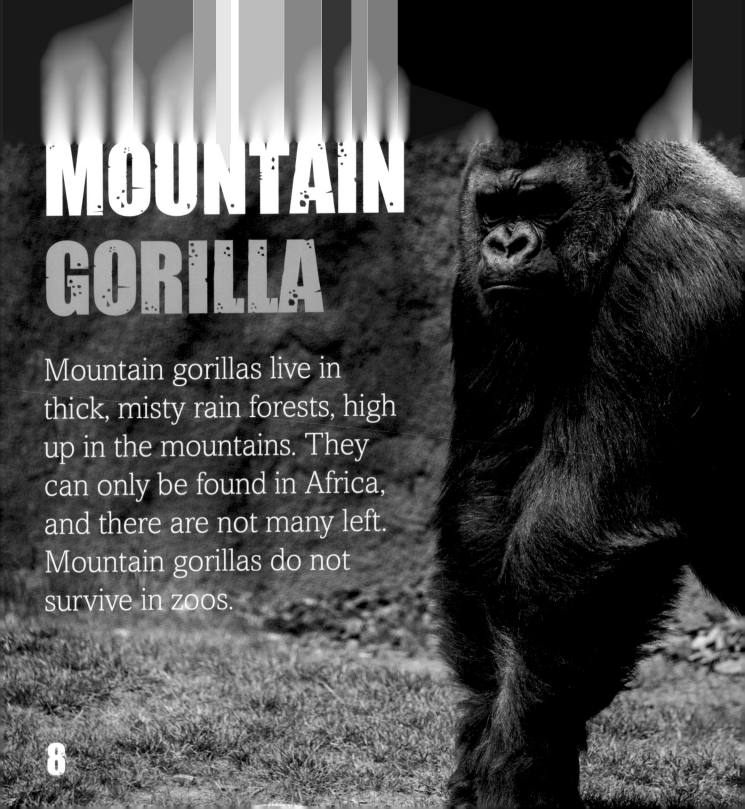

MOUNTAIN GORILLA

Mountain gorillas live in thick, misty rain forests, high up in the mountains. They can only be found in Africa, and there are not many left. Mountain gorillas do not survive in zoos.

One of the reasons that the number of mountain gorillas has become so small is that, for a long time, they were hunted by people. More recently, their habitats have been cut down for extra land for farming. The **remaining** gorillas live in protected parks, where **rangers** work hard to keep them safe.

THE OCEAN

Almost three-quarters of the world's surface is covered in salty water. There are five main oceans, and the Pacific Ocean is the largest. The oceans are extremely important; they even affect the weather. Below the oceans, minerals and oil can be found.

Oceans are home to some of the largest and the smallest creatures on the planet, including whales, dolphins, sea turtles, and fish.

DID YOU KNOW THAT THOUSANDS OF BIRDS RELY ON THE OCEANS FOR THEIR FOOD?

THE BLUE WHALE

Whales are large mammals that live in the sea. There are 83 whale species in the world. Blue whales are the largest of all whales. Blue whales can be found in deep oceans all over the world.

More than half of young blue whales die because they are not strong enough to swim in rough water or they are killed by killer whales. People used to hunt blue whales, which has decreased the number of blue whales in the ocean.

A KILLER WHALE

POLLUTION IN THE OCEAN IS A DANGER TO WHALES, TOO.

13

THE AFRICAN SAVANNA

A savanna is a large area of grassland. Savannas have large amounts of trees, but, unlike forests, the trees are scattered around. There are two seasons in the African savanna: the dry season and the wet season.

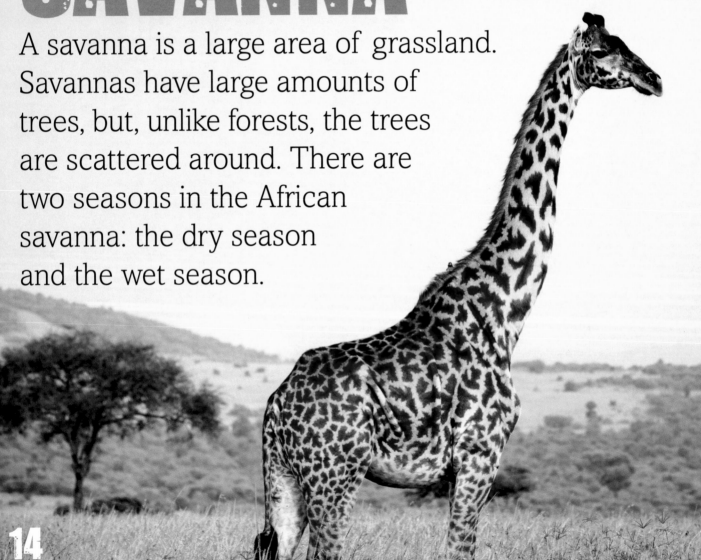

Many animals can be found living on the plains of Africa, including giraffes, zebras, and cheetahs. During the dry season, these animals can struggle to find water and must be careful to avoid waiting crocodiles!

PLANTS LIVING IN A SAVANNA MUST BE ABLE TO WITHSTAND LONG PERIODS WITHOUT WATER.

15

THE AFRICAN ELEPHANT

The African elephant is the largest animal on land. There are two types of African elephants. The savanna elephant is the largest. Elephants need a large amount of space; they can **roam** areas of up to 11,580 square miles (30,000 sq km).

The population of African elephants has **decreased**. Some people choose to kill elephants for their ivory tusks. These people are called poachers. Ivory is used to make jewelry and can be ground down to make medicine.

TUSKS

POACHERS SELL THE IVORY IN ORDER TO MAKE MONEY. ELEPHANTS' MEAT AND SKIN ARE ALSO SOLD.

THE ARCTIC

The Arctic is located in the most northern part of Earth, making it very cold. Much of the area is covered in thick ice, depending on the time of year. The Arctic region is made up of the Arctic Ocean and parts of Canada, Russia, the United States, Greenland, Norway, Finland, Sweden, and Iceland.

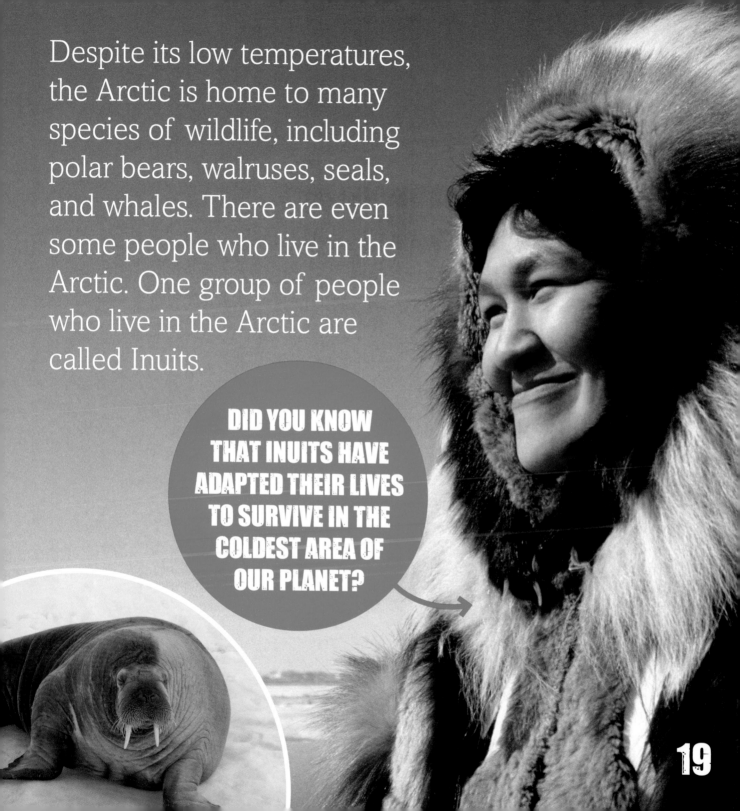

Despite its low temperatures, the Arctic is home to many species of wildlife, including polar bears, walruses, seals, and whales. There are even some people who live in the Arctic. One group of people who live in the Arctic are called Inuits.

DID YOU KNOW THAT INUITS HAVE ADAPTED THEIR LIVES TO SURVIVE IN THE COLDEST AREA OF OUR PLANET?

THE POLAR BEAR

The polar bear is a close relative to the brown bear. The polar bear lives in the Arctic, and, although it is born on land, it spends much of its life in the water. Polar bears are **carnivorous**, mainly eating seals and fish.

For some time, polar bears were hunted by humans, which led to a large decrease in their population. Now protected, the largest threat to polar bears is climate change. As the world gradually warms up, the ice of the Arctic melts, leaving the polar bear with less habitat in which to hunt.

OTHER ENDANGERED ANIMALS

Unfortunately, there are many other animals on our planet that are also at risk.

There are only a few black rhinos left, and the western black rhino is now extinct. Black rhinos are largely in danger due to poachers killing them for their horns.

The snow leopard is being hunted for its rare, beautiful fur; it is now nearing extinction.

Many of the forests where orangutans live have been made into farms. There have also been **severe** forest fires, which have made life for orangutans very difficult.

The northern bald ibis vanished from Europe almost completely in the 17th century because people hunted it for food.

GLOSSARY

carnivorous	meat-eating
decreased	got smaller
extinct	completely wiped out
rangers	people who work to protect an area of land
remaining	left over when other parts are gone
roam	wander freely
severe	serious

INDEX